A Crown

for

Ted and Sylvia

A CROWN
FOR
TED AND SYLVIA

Kim Bridgford

RESOURCE *Publications* • Eugene, Oregon

A CROWN FOR TED AND SYLVIA

Resource Publications
An Imprint of Wipf and Stock Publishers
199 W. 8th Ave., Suite 3
Eugene, OR 97401

www.wipfandstock.com

PAPERBACK ISBN: 978-1-5326-7288-0
HARDCOVER ISBN: 978-1-5326-7289-7
EBOOK ISBN: 978-1-5326-7290-3

Manufactured in the U.S.A.   JULY 5, 2019

Cover Image: Ted Hughes & Sylvia Plath in Yorkshire, England, 1956.
Photograph by Harry Patrick Ogden.
Courtesy of Smith College Special Collections

Ruth Fainlight Letter: *The Letters of Sylvia Plath*, Volume II, pp. 658-59.

This book is for everyone who has ever been fascinated by the work of Sylvia Plath and Ted Hughes. Even now, over forty years after reading *The Bell Jar*, I am still in love—and so I offer up this crown.

Friday 6 October 1961

Dear Ruth (Fainlight),

A small note to say you are an angel for the terrific apple recipes & how I hope you are all right. It's difficult & in a way impertinent to tell you how very much I am wishing things to go well for you, because noone can ever really identify deeply enough with someone else's special predicament to make the words "I know how you feel" carry their full weight . . .

Lots of love,
Sylvia

Contents

Permissions

The American Journal of Poetry:"Nick Hughes"
"Potboiler"

The Christian Century:"Karma"
"Lazarus"
"Peter"
"You Can't Go Back"

Crab Orchard Review:"Over the Hill"
"Why People in Their Fifties Read Mystery Books"

Crannog:"A Pentina for My Leopard Coat"

The Cresset:"Judas"

Light:"Martian Landing, Fishtown"

Lighten Up:"Fool's Gold"
"Hillary Clinton"
"Jennifer Lawrence"

Literary Matters:"The Artist"

The Lyric:"What Fresh Hell Is This?"

The Moth:"Martian Intermarriage in Philadelphia"

Peacock Journal:"Spoils"
"Why Sisyphus Isn't a Woman"

Plath Profiles:"Buying Sylvia Plath's Typewriter"
"A Crown for Ted and Sylvia"

Raintown Review:"Brides of Christ"

The Rotary Dial: "Jesus Is God's Selfie"

I am grateful to the following journal editors, who have brought my work to print: Melissa Balmain and Kevin Durkin; Dolores Mildred Batten, Julia Gordon Bramer, William Buckley, and Robert Eric Shoemaker; Jill Pelaez Baumgartner; Jerome Betts; Sarah Bunting, Tony O'Dwyer, Ger Burke, and Jarlath Fahy; Pino Coluccio and Alexandra Oliver; Anna Evans; Marci Johnson; Allison Joseph and Jon Tribble; Bill and Kate Lantry; Robert Nazarene; Rebecca O'Connor; and Ryan Wilson. I wish to thank them for the tireless work they do to support writers.

"J. R. R. Tolkien" and "Donald Trump" appeared in *Higgledy Piggledy*, edited by Daniel Groves and Greg Williamson (Waywiser Press).

"The Death of Sylvia Plath's Father," under the title "Loving Otto Plath," appeared in *Love Affairs at the Villa Nelle*, edited by Marilyn L. Taylor and James P. Roberts (Kelsay Books).

"A Pentina for My Leopard Coat" was included in the *Crannog* launch on Friday, June 29, 2018, in Galway, Ireland.

"Trump's Seven Forbidden Words" appeared in the CDC Project, edited by Sarah Freligh and Amy Lemmon.

"Why Emily Dickinson Would March on Washington" appeared in *Nasty Women Poets*, edited by Grace Bauer and Julie Kane (Lost Horse Press).

I.

A Crown for Ted and Sylvia

A Crown for Ted and Sylvia

1. The Reader

You never know the truth, but try to guess.
You dream a farm of moon-lit wolves and foxes.
The oven makes you pause: the inside boxes
Of a marriage. Hard to say who is most jealous,
Hungry for the clapping literati.
What do you have to give up? Put on offer?
What ancient spirit is the ruling cipher?
The profits from *The Bell Jar* make the party.

Now everyone is dead but Frieda,
But still there is the context, and the rope,
And Nicholas hanging down. Inside a
Family it is terrible; the soap
Of the concentration camp, the gas
That sickens you as it will come to pass.

2. Sylvia

What sickens you as it will come to pass?
Hindsight sifting the rubble, the relics.

Electro-shock. The other schizophrenics
Making lambs of paper plates. Your choice

Was to write.

           I want to be a god.
It is not that I want to be dead. I want perfection.
Assia's kiss something I saw, the kitchen
Dirty now. I backed away from Ted.

And there were more, and there had always been.
I wanted to will the world into my own.
I didn't like it, terrified or cold.
It was ruined. You can't go back, then.
Betrayal nibbled there, along my bone.
It was inside that kiss that I grew old.

3. Ted

It was inside that kiss that I grew bold.
Sometimes there is relief. No one to see
(Except, it seems, my wife). Sometimes, a beauty
Is inevitable. Maude Gonne. Yeats failed,
But his poetry would make his singing name.
I wanted everything. A language. Awe.
I wanted the insides of what I saw.
And so I left. There was a separate room

For Sylvia, and also for Assia.
Not too many people know a third.
So the world can be. I was dividing.
I didn't see my conscience as an idea,
But rather as a way inside the word.
When Sylvia died, I was in hiding.

4. Olwyn, Ted's Sister

When Sylvia died, I was, in hating
Her already, an unexpected state.
Bitch. Like Barbie on a primal date,
She choreographed what we'd all be wading
Through for life: *her* life, *her* observations.
Like Virginia Woolf, she made the money
That paid for everything. It was like honey,
Her papers and her poems. Shrewd. Way stations

To the dead. Meanwhile, I watched the children grow:
To school, *tra-la-la*. It is hard to be the story
Of a ghost, of people's own vague narratives.
It seemed it wrote itself long time ago.
I loved Ted too. I am not really sorry.
You tell yourself the story as it lives.

5. Shura, Ted's Daughter with Assia

You tell yourself the story as it lives,
And mine was that my mother was as dead
As I was. You see, we lived inside the head
Of Sylvia, and because she had her sheaves
Of manuscripts, then, doubled, so would we.
I was four when I died, and I was "one up,"
The child who died, a pretty buttercup,
Along with Mother. This, too, is family.

There are things that I would like to have done,
But sometimes you're a prop, or almost placed
To give dramatic contrast to the act.
We were more than Sylvia, the one
Who was two, the one who was twice blessed.
We were an undeniable fact.

6. Nicholas

We were an undeniable fact,
And we were a fiction, in other words, a family.
I was a baby, both Ted Hughes and Plath:
And Otto too. From genealogy,
The traits could re-connect, for all we knew,
But something else as well. A mythic true.
I had a well inside that I'd look down,
Like sorrow's fetus, opening. No sound

The day I killed myself. I was my mother
Without her fame, but I would know the loss
Of ambition hurling down, with vicious seething.
I was, in the end, a version of her father.
My hanging was ancestral. All our eyes.
In a row, we are our silent voices mouthing.

7. Aurelia

In a row we are our silent voices mouthing.
I want to be last. As the official word,
I want the world to know my girl was good.
I don't want people thinking of her breathing
Out these lies. I want the smart and normal,
The one who would do anything for Mother.
I want to take the rights back from the father.
She was sad then. She cooked. She shaped a formal

Way that everything was going to be.
I didn't like that she was cruel about
The things I did. But either way, I bless.
My goal is to control her legacy.
It doesn't matter in her winding sheet:
You never know the truth, but try to guess.

Buying Sylvia Plath's Typewriter

I want the words to burn. So too the ribbon,
Like a silken extension, or like betrayal's braid.
Words have a power—although not quite as often
As we hope—to throw the Underworld some shade.
They thought of themselves as gods, the best gods going,
But gods that could type—and would—and saw themselves
As makers of a special brand of knowing.
They'd place themselves with spirits. Who resolves
To live in rural landscapes? These two.
                                          The keys
Today are quaint with fire. The time has passed
Where people think relationships can last.
I'm an optimist by nature, hurt by lies.
The more I use this typewriter, I will learn
Through simple practice how the world can burn.

Sylvia Plath's Paper Dolls

If Sylvia's paper dolls were to play with mine,
It would be crazy. Each change in an idea
Would be narrated by rule maker Sylvia.
That would be the only way to break a line.

My dolls were lovely too. I used their tabs
To hold on tight, to turn my back on terror.
(By that I mean, of course, potential error.)
I like to think that Sylvia's mad libs

Of poems were what I, too, was trying to say.
My paper dolls are not in museums, but lost
To history, burned, or turned to dust.
I remember when Sylvia, still ordinary,

Created who she was through paper scraps.
That's how we terrorize ourselves. Cuts. Snips.

That Sylvia Plath Feeling

So many of us wanted to be her;
So many of us wanted to be famous:
So many of us the inheritor.

What we didn't want: to go so far.
What we didn't want, *not the same as.*
So many of us wanted to be her:

But without Ted, without the madness card,
Without her daddy, blackboard showbiz,
So many of us the inheritor

Of typing up the manuscripts, the professor
Grading papers: "It is what it is."
So many of us wanted to be her.

We thought we could be good *and* ruthless. Are
Good and ruthless poets in the skies?
So many of us the inheritor,

Looking for the combination to be her
And yet without depression and surprise:
So many of us wanted to be her,
So many of us the inheritor.

Greater Than or Less Than

Like us, she wanted to be good and true. Like us,
She wanted to be perfect, dedicated.
She wanted trauma too, enough to break us.

She would go all the way. Where it would take us
Was more than a boat, capsized, now empty, righted.
Like us, she wanted to be good and true. Like us,

She wanted to outdo the structure, premise.
She wanted it so much she would die for it.
She wanted trauma too. Enough to break us

Was just her getting started. Doubting Thomas,
She'd put her hand in, to understand it.
Like us, she wanted to be good and true. Like us,

She waited for the Publishers Clearing House
To declare her winnings. She knew she had won it.
She wanted trauma too. Enough to break us

Was the oven on, and breathing in the gas.
We balked, and took her sacrifice for granted.
Like us, she wanted to be good and true. Like us,
She wanted trauma too—and so broke us.

Winning

She didn't like it when she didn't win.
She was a realist and self-promotor.
She'd dominate each friendly competition:

Art, writing, camp; the sherry hour, new fashion.
People were taken aback. Not mediocre,
She didn't like it when she didn't win.

Ruthless and clear-eyed, she found the metered line
Had backing from the poets there before her.
She'd dominate each friendly competition

Because, for her, it took place with tradition
(And with the fawning of a courtier).
She didn't like it. When she didn't win,

She didn't have the money, or the ribbon,
Just the loss. What purpose was left to her?
She didn't like it when she didn't win,

So spent her life eyeing a clear solution.
She gassed herself. The laurel crowning there,
She didn't like it when she didn't win.
She'd dominate each friendly competition.

Whose Story Is It Anyway?

So many times we do not know the truth.
So many times we just have an idea.
We shape what's left into a useful myth.

For instance, we mistook whom Ted was with,
Which is why no one could find him with Assia.
So many times we do not know the truth,

But improvise. Such is the courtier's oath.
We use our indignation. Nick and Frieda!
We shape what's left into a useful myth.

Protagonist: wronged Sylvia. A laugh
From Hawthorne's woods discovers Shura.
So many times we do not know the truth.

We parse what's left: separated, off
In Yeats's house. Another gyre and era.
We shape what's left into a useful myth.

Assia upped the competition path
By killing Shura too, increasing terror.
So many times we do not know the truth.
We shape what's left into a useful myth.

Ted Hughes

Let's shift the tale, and start with Frieda, or
We start with Nick, or perhaps with Shura.
It's not as interesting, absent myth and drama.
It's best to start with suicidal mama.

Divorce is sad. Your tale is now rewritten.
The narrative, made up of pink and satin,
Now sold in a garage sale. Colossal fail
When what you saw as epic has turned stale.

Drab that: and strange. With nothing as it was,
You can't get back your magic, lit showbiz.
Better to rewrite the shorter, cleaner arc.
No one has to know it didn't work.

You couldn't have anticipated Ted
Could not escape the story. Maybe you did.

Disneyland

The first Disneyland opened July 17, 1955,
and was a disaster because of counterfeited tickets;
Sylvia Plath and Ted Hughes married 1956.

It's not that she was masochistic and
He was not. They both chose '50s roles.
They were human in their Disneyland,

But thought they were outside. They had it planned,
Although he had the predatory goals.
It's not that she was masochistic and

He was sado-. No. In nature, cycles twined
Together. Rabbits scurried down their holes.
They were human. Call it Disneyland.

Call it living life as artists. Call it mind
Over natter. Working on the office goals
It's not. That she was masochistic and

He was not was an oversimplification.
Together they would rule. In hills and dales,
They were human in their Disneyland,

While being well aware that they would find
Others: women, temptations. Summing up their styles,
It's not that she was masochistic. Weaned,
They were human in their Disneyland.

Owl

Predatory too, she was like an owl,
Turning her head, dandelion eerie.
She fed on others: poets, language, fowl.

That's how you're supposed to do it. Not *steal*
Exactly: the shadow like a sound. The eye
Predatory too, she was like an owl,

And wearing her own mystery, like a cowl,
She honed in: taking what had flickered by.
She fed on others: poets, language, fowl.

That's what happens. Ur-permissible,
She'd take Yeats and golden artistry,
Predatory too. She was like an owl,

Creating a vicious tableau. As for her soul,
She could harm or please, all for the story.
She fed on others: poets, language, fowl.

The texture was like scritching in a bowl;
You throw up what you don't need, gory,
Predatory too. She was like an owl
Feeding on others: poets, language, fowl.

Frieda and Nicholas

Her name means "peaceful ruler," his "victory
Of the people." How strange these naming rites.
Frieda is still alive, but Nicholas would die.

They set a course of action. Truth or lie,
They made their own from these linguistic fates.
Her name means "peaceful ruler," his "victory

Of the people." Together, they were history:
They woke up, startled, in the house of Yeats.
Frieda is still alive, but Nicholas would die

Years later in Alaska, looking away
From people gouging out his name. In plots,
Her name means "peaceful ruler," his "victory."

At times, another needs a clue, or key.
It has nothing to do with children's rights.
Frieda is still alive, but Nicholas would die,

Some would say like Otto, out of self-pity.
Others would say, out of ancestral rights.
Her name means "peaceful ruler," his "victory":
Frieda is still alive, but Nicholas would die.

Nick Hughes

who died by hanging

By then, you thought your best was second rate:
Because it's always all of it: the headstones
Chipped to take off "Hughes." It was your birthright.
You had to start with both your parents' lines.

A scientist, a child who moved away,
You were more Otto Plath than Sylvia,
More Ted. Yet all of them were there. Your lie
Was that it was just you, in Alaska,
Good at what you did, but not a god.

Sometimes ordinariness is not enough.
If you were to make a list of what you did,
It would be small, and sometimes people, off
The grid, refuse the grind of daily plod.
You knew, of course, you could not be yourself.

The Death of Sylvia Plath's Father

She couldn't understand her father gone,
Or why he'd leave her. She was only eight.
She thought it cruel—and that, in death, he'd won.

No matter where she was, she meant to win
Him back. She chose the archetypal fight.
She couldn't understand her father gone.

The structures are not anything but pattern:
They're not imbued with love, or tears, or sight.
She thought it cruel—and that, in death, he'd won.

She didn't understand the answer written;
Her re-interpretation was her fate.
She couldn't understand her father gone.

So pretended he was there. History's rewritten
All the time. Her mortal life was cold with granite.
She thought it cruel—and that, in death, he'd won.

She practiced as if for a competition,
And so it was: she'd not be second-rate.
She couldn't understand her father gone.
She thought it cruel—and that, in death, she'd won.

Potboiler

Remember that they weren't enough at first.
Remember that it took the literati.
Remember that the myth rewrote the worst.

Wife sends out her husband's manuscripts? Pierced
By gender, the word is *anonymity.*
Remember that they weren't enough. At first,

It was the script, although those lines were cursed.
You had to be in love, there at the party.
Remember that the myth rewrote the worst:

Assia-style. They never were divorced:
She the Smith professor-secretary.
Remember that they weren't enough at first.

The Bell Jar was their ticket, money nursed.
Sylvia was Philomena Guinea.
Remember that the myth rewrote the worst.

In ironies of life they were well versed.
Her potboiler the legacy and money.
Remember that they weren't enough at first.
Remember that the myth rewrote the worst.

Sylvia and Assia

Sylvia

I did all the things I was supposed to do.
Reward: maternal love; book publication.
Whatever happens, I can outlast you.

Assia

I was pretty as a coin, a city tableau.
So many times, I offered up a Helen.
I did all the things. I was supposed to do . . .

Sylvia

Something different. Not an in-the-know
Kiss across the dish towel. My caution:
Whatever happens, I can outlast you.

Assia

I wanted admiration, offered Shura too.
To double would erase the gas and oven.
I did all the things I was supposed to do.

Sylvia

But your writing wasn't good enough. You're through.
A worker bee, I had Plan B in motion.
Whatever happens, I can outlast you:

Because I had *The Bell Jar. Entre nous,*
It helps to have a back-up; in my fiction,
I did. All the things I was supposed to do?
Whatever happens, I can outlast you.

And Then Frieda Became a Bereavement Counselor

When Frieda became a bereavement counselor,
Everything seemed right. The family dead,
Now she could control what happened, with a prayer.

Now she could unloose myth, beneath the door,
The children both asleep, who had inherited.
When Frieda became a bereavement counselor,

It was still *in medias res*, ongoing war;
Sylvia Plath was dead, her story edited.
Now she could control what happened. With a prayer,

She wished upon her mother's birthing star,
Somebody else's dream reconstituted.
When Frieda became a bereavement counselor.

It was not a question of *him* or of *her*:
It was the way the sorrow was distributed.
Now she could control what happened. With a prayer

Or a poem, or with a two-year-old's lost mother,
She'd bring the world's lost sorrow to a head.
When Frieda became a bereavement counselor,
Now she could control what happened, with a prayer.

II.

Vertigo

Kim Novak and Sammy Davis, Jr.

You belonged to them, as much as you said no,
As much as you lived in your beach house, as much
As you said, "You won't control where I stay or go."

But that's not how those things work. So and so
Meets so and so. So! It was your human touch:
You belonged to them, as much as you said no.

Was it comedian meets ingénue?
Was it black and white keys? That no one would watch?
You said, "You won't control where I stay or go."

Yet, the times were such, and not so long ago,
That a sham marriage was not thought overmuch.
You belonged to them, as much as you said no.

As much as you say it doesn't matter, though,
Your time is gone. In that one moment's clutch,
You said, "You won't control where I stay or go."

Of course, you were right. Of course, it's nothing new.
Still, you'd like to do it over, Mr. Such and Such.
You belonged to them, as much as you said no.
You said, "You won't control where I stay or go."

Kim Novak, Sixty Years After *Vertigo*

I was nothing like you, but I watched.
I loved your tragedy with Scottie.
Years later, you commented as you etched:

How you were made. First you were sketched,
As Hitchcock always did. Then you were ready.
I was nothing like you, but I watched.

Your private life did not concern them. Cached,
Your personality was there for Sammy.
Years later, you commented as you etched,

Scottie, climbing the ladder, flushed.
Your character was beautiful and empty.
I was nothing like you, but I watched.

So many things untrue: but molded, niched,
That men can look to when they're feeling needy.
Years later, you commented as you etched,

Sixty years after your true meaning botched.
Leaping from the tower made you heady.
I was nothing like you, but I watched.
Years later, you commented as you etched.

The Tower

You don't want people feeling sorry for you.
You want to be alone. How hard that is!
The circumstances got the best of you.

He was funny: you laughed. That's how Jane Doe
Was lost: you snuggled up to showbiz.
You don't want people feeling sorry for you.

And not to say that you had vertigo,
No. It's just that love is what it is.
The circumstances got the best of you,

And it's so rare in life that that is true.
Think about it. And then it's nobody's business.
You don't want people feeling sorry for you.

In the tower shadow, you cried, *No, no, no,*
And fell. You put your life inside the pause.
The circumstances got the best of you.

Because, of course, the things they said were true.
You loved him. You could be true, not wise.
You don't want people feeling sorry for you.
The circumstances got the best of you.

III.

Pentinas

A Pentina for My Leopard Coat

I love everything about my old leopard coat:
Its style, its softness, and its vintage Calvin look.
(It made me buy another one, this year, in blond.)
It makes me strangely feel more loved, more desired,
As silly as that might sound. I feel like an animal.

One time, an owner, with an actual animal,
Told me that his dog was attracted to my coat.
For that reason—that my outerwear was desired—
The owner kept walking with me. *Look, look,*
He said. I did. The dog was beautiful and blond.

It happens everywhere. Bald, brunette, blond:
Nice coat! Sometimes they ask which animal,
And someone, once, complimented my hair, my look.
If you have a good haircut and a good coat,
What else matters? Laughed. Like a child desired,

I don't want to take off my coat. Leopard—desired
In my house—grew to pajamas, another coat (blond),
A dress and jacket. It all comes back to my ur-coat.
Perhaps this is the reason I don't buy an animal:
Perhaps, one day, I am afraid that people won't look.

Sometimes, when I get my hair cut, to get my look,
My stylist laughs. She believes my coat story, desired
Along with my haircut. *They think you're an animal.*
No, no, I say. When I ask if I should be blond,
She says the same. *No, no.* It is that damned leopard coat.

Meanwhile, to be desired, I dream of the blond coat.
But I haven't worn it. It doesn't look like my spirit-animal.

A Pentina for Antarctica

When I think of Antarctica, I think of Adelie penguins.
Today, I found out 1.5 million of them were hidden,
Which is easy to do, contrary to expectations, in the ice.
Still, it's hard for me to keep a secret, let alone
Hide penguins, thought almost extinct, upon an island.

Of course, we compartmentalize too—we don't say island—
We call them problems, or our bad side, not our penguins.
That's how we feel better and still good when we're alone.
However, if you're Adelie, you would prefer to be literal, hidden,
Even in such numbers—whatever you have to do—on the ice.

Because, to be quite frank, it's the predators on the ice:
Humans, rats, cats, anything that shouldn't be on the island,
Stealing the eggs, tagging the skins, using the net (hidden),
And, over time, it's like whales and elephants. The penguins
Do what they have to do to survive, replicate, be alone

With their other almost 1.5 million friends. Left alone,
They can focus on business, relax, not be once, twice
Shy. They can define what it means to be penguins.
And, if they don't like this one, they can choose another island,
Just sail off on some sheet ice, re-write the definition of hidden.

With global warming, that might not be long. To be hidden
Is to be your own personality, to trick yourself into being alone
With the rest of the population. Each penguin is an island;
Each penguin tells the story of the Adelie on Antarctic ice.
It has to feel personal, though, to be yourself in all the penguins.

It's like hunting for hidden pictures of Adelie penguins:
Once you see them, they are plain as ice, alone, on an island.

A Pentina for the Star

Of course, I'm thinking about this after the Oscars, one star
Here, one star there, and I think, This is an extravaganza
Really (not that that's news). What if we moved the show
To something else? Poetry, chess, Scrabble, jacks, alcohol.
This is like one of those games on Facebook: sports vs. teachers.

It is supposed to be a hoot, although the joke hurts teachers.
Because we like glam, sparkles, big names, not one little star
At the top of the page. Because we are fans of alcohol
And, as much as we protest to the contrary, an extravaganza.
It's the same with stars in the sky: we like the really big show.

Every time the weather changes, it has to be a big deal, a show,
So that at 4 a.m. we are lined up getting groceries, with teachers,
Who already have to set their alarms to 5:00. An extravaganza
Of toilet paper, and milk, and bread. By 8:00 the weather star
Is on, sheepish, saying that it was just a scare. Some alcohol

Is what people need right now. But it's too early for alcohol,
And people are working, although some people are no-show
Because of the warning. *Oh, everyday people, don't you want a star?
The day so drab, undone, before you?* The inspiration of teachers
Is not enough. Some days, you wake up, want an extravaganza,

However that's displayed. You want the Broadway extravaganza,
The Oscars, the rowboat on the water, sipping your flask of alcohol,
Looking at the fireworks, thinking, I finally know what my teachers
Were saying. In wonder, each night, in bed, we watch the show,
Eyelids closed, dreaming. When I think about how to be a star,

This is what keeps me going, alcohol of knowing: the show.
Teachers, from the first, you said the extravaganza was a star.

A Pentina for Erasure

Sometimes it is what is missing that you want, regardless
Of its value. It just means, really, you can't remember
What it was, and so it takes on the tint of nostalgia,
Something with a sepia fragrance and wayfarer tone.
Sometimes you are just saying that you are alone.

Not that being alone is bad. It is just that being alone
Makes you more like a number, or entity, regardless
Of your purpose or intention. It adjusts your tone.
You want the most that you can really remember,
And, if not, you'll make it up: that is nostalgia.

When you were little, you didn't understand nostalgia:
You thought it was a version of now, being alone
With yourself. You didn't understand that, to remember,
You have to erase, you have to rewrite, regardless
Of the truth. Each person has an individual tone.

For example, when I think of childhood, its soft tone,
It doesn't have anything to do with me, that nostalgia,
And it informs everything I do. So it is, regardless.
The past is like the pronoun "it": sitting there alone,
Inviting others to interpret it. You try to remember

What you were trying to say. Who can remember?
In any event, it has a glow, it has a shape and tone.
When you are older, by yourself, living there alone,
You understand the viewpoint is purely nostalgia:
All of it, from your kitchen chair, thinking, regardless

Of any other tactic, regardless of your coffee or tone,
Regardless of what you remember, other than being alone.

A Pentina for the Number Five

All I can think about is five these days. Five sides, five reasons,
Five dollars off. If five is my world view, are there spells
That involve five? What five things in a Shakespeare play—
Besides the meter—would bring about a marriage or death?
When I was a child, learning my times tables, I loved five,

How money, stars, pentagons, crime stories, brought me to five
Dollars, even fifty. I still love the rhythm of it, all the reasons
We clean out our wallets, to look for more. Building wealth, not death,
Or debt is the key. At the same time, I need poetry for the spells,
For the magic of the word and soul, for church, for the mouth-play.

It's funny. We talk about the weather, sports, politics. Why not play
With something else: move to the intimacy of literature, five
Favorite books, dreams in the dark, hope? What finally spells
Meaning or ending? Once, as a child, I sat on the porch, reasons
In my pretend bag of tricks, and I tried to conjure animals—death

Or life, I was not discriminate. I wanted the glass unicorn of death,
The shiny transparency of desire. I wanted what would play
In every lit landscape, every tiny town, with its own cicada-reasons.
Later that summer, a horse died on the highway. It was five
Minutes later that the landscape was red and howling. Spells

Can do that. Even now, I desire to look through the book of spells,
And they could be anything, from a way to avoid sudden death,
To love. When my husband had a heart attack, he tried five
Different methods to stop what was happening. The final play
Worked: a nurse running him down the hall, like hell. Reasons

To live, finally, are reasons enough. My favorite spells
Are not about death. They play with chant and end with five.

A Pentina for Fake Love

How late am I to the party? Fake love. Fake motives.
My son told me not to look at online dating sites, make a website
Where people could get together. What? You wouldn't believe
What people will do. So hold on to purity like a piece of velvet,
Although sometimes you'll be lonely, sometimes you'll want to talk,

Sometimes you will want to go out to eat, have a drink, small talk,
But in a 1950s script. I am always surprised at ulterior motives,
Even this far in my life. I still want to wear a dress that's velvet
With a cameo. I want a rotary phone, a candle, and no website.
Maybe this is *all* fake. Maybe, whatever it is, you want to believe

In something other than yourself. For instance, my son will believe
In each new app as a sifter of the world. When GrubHub, the talk
Of the town, brings ice cream and soda pop, I want the pre-website
World, to wit, walking; to wit, the restaurant. These are other motives,
I realize. For my son, writing music, the nighttime world like velvet,

It is nice to have a snack in the middle of the night. I made a velvet
Dress, years ago, as a home ec project—in fact, the whole doll. To believe
In the gift of the doll to a nursery school! I had pureheart motives,
But, when I went to visit the school, I saw the doll, wrecked, no talk
Of fixing her. I have always believed in the world, not the website,

Even though, these days, that is almost foolish, the anti-website.
I'm all right. I'm like Miss Emily, surrounded by old values and velvet:
Just call me Miss Kim. These individual worlds are lonely. No talk,
Just a nostalgia Christmas tree wheel turning the lights, to believe
In something beyond the regular. You see, I need lofty motives,

Whether or not they work. Velvet, and pearls, and stories: to believe
Is to live outside a website. Whether or not you talk, you have motives.

IV.

Jesus Is God's Selfie

Fool's Gold

(on reading a faux internet story)

ATLANTA LOTTERY WINNER DIES
AFTER GOLD PLATING HIS TESTICLES

"The human body is not made to
handle being gold-plated," said Dr. Rife.
"I don't care how much money you have."

What do you do when a hundred million calls?
Go on vacation? Buy a house a two?
You want to be creative, use your balls.

There are those for whom this fantasy appalls.
They say you're drunk, that you'll never follow through.
What do you do when a hundred million calls?

You follow an impulse like Niagara Falls.
You do what people tell you not to do,
With an automotive plater. You have the balls.

You'll do this thing to your own testicles.
It is the Midas touch without a clue.
What do you do when a hundred million calls?

You lose your mind. At first, the golden swells
Delight you: but it is passion, not I.Q.,
That forms the narrative of golden balls.

Oh sure, it seems apocryphal. Like golden bells,
They ring to caution things you should not do.
When destiny, with its golden finger, calls,
The answer, Watson? Don't think with your balls.

Donald Trump

Higgledy-piggledy
Donald Phallacious
Brings back elections
To Homecoming court.

No time for subtlety
(Hit-on-the-headery):
Just calls to greatness
And not to abort.

Trump's Seven Forbidden Words

Who would object to any one of these—
Science-based, diversity, and *fetus*—
It's like when you're polite, but don't say please

(What difference, really, does it make)? The lies—
Entitlement and *vulnerable*—hit us.
Who would object to any one of these:

Evidence-based, transgender? OEDs
Reassert themselves from Wiki-itus.
It's like when you're polite, but don't say please

(The way that we train all our PhDs).
But acquiescence will come back to bite us.
Who would object to any one of these?

Beware the military soft surprise:
It's language first. So pretty, they can shoot us.
It's like when you're polite, but don't say please.

They say that it's a shower. Such naïfs!
You offer up yourself to barracudas.
Who would object to any one of these?
It's like when you're polite, but don't say please.

Hillary Clinton

Higgledy-piggledy
Hillary Clinton
Breaks the glass ceiling
In multiple ways.

Some wouldn't stand for
The world matriarchal;
Others find hope
In the pantsuit that slays.

Why Emily Dickinson Would March on Washington

Unsuffocate—release Before—
Because some things you leave home for.

With more than jam—and You are ready
Because sometimes a basket's heavy.

Because your dashes work—away—
Because you have a door—Cachet—

Because you find you write to sew
Both Life—and death. You have to go.

Jennifer Lawrence

Higgledy piggledy
Jennifer Lawrence
Red carpet tripping
Academy crowns.

We like to laugh at
Women's-Tom-shoe-ery.
But let's see a man
Wear one of those gowns.

Taylor Swift

Higgledy Piggledy
Taylor Swiftmania
Surges when she files a
Suit for a touch.

Don't put your hand
On-her-back-part-i-a,
Claim it's her waistline
When it's her tush.

J. R. R. Tolkien

Higgledy-piggledy
J. R. R. Tolkien
Lost in a landscape
Of trees, hills, and dales.

So much time given to
Rings-that-are-Precious:
Better to stop this
And just go to Zale's.

Martian Landing, Fishtown

And then what if they moved into row houses?
In this old-fashioned, ethnic neighborhood,
The ship, like cymbals pulled apart, would set
The three-eyed Martians down, their slender voices
Chittering like squirrels or background noises.
They'd be the quiet neighbors: '50s odd.
Before long, they'd know: "How are you today?",
And cover their third eye with a beret.

In any event, they'd like the neighborhood.
Hip. Better food. A younger, tattooed vibe.
Eventually, they'd start a Martian trend.
I've heard that they prefer to eat what's found
In green things: avocado, broccoli rabe.
The real estate's gone up. The music's good.

Martian Intermarriage in Philadelphia

Like all such unions, the beginning is the hardest.
The antennae! The green bodies! The three eyes!
But love requires no prototype, and tries
To make of daily life what was absurdist.

The children are so sweet! Light green and smart.
Sometimes in newborns the pulsating heart
Draws metal things to it, like nails and spoons.
There is an easy fix, the doctor intones.

Your child is not a magnet. You call the tune.
They hang their heads. Of course. A neon smile
Reminds a tourist of the crocodile.
A glow-in-the-dark flicker made while molting:
A Tinder characteristic that's unfolding.
A generation passes, and they swoon.

Jesus Is God's Selfie

Seen on a T-Shirt for Sale in a Window

Because it was inevitable, for God
Knows everything—not only pain and love
But Facebook, iPhones, all technology—
Jesus would become his father's selfie.

It makes sense, really: an earthly view of God
To share. The awe of light makes you believe.
Those posing by Kardashians or Jay-Z,
Adele and Taylor Swift, or Bey,

Have nothing on the son of God. How many
Times can *this* be posted on a wall?
And just like Jesus will reflect his father,
So those who stand with him will sound the call.
"Like," "like," they click. Around the earth they travel,
The "likes" of love, of all the tongues together.

V.

What Fresh Hell Is This?

Lazarus

Fishers of men

Because you found me somewhere in-between,
Because you realized the truth of that,
You pulled me up. The not-seen was now seen—

Like something that's half-buried, serpentine,
A vine the wind has covered, dust unset—
Because you found me. Somewhere in-between,

The insects covered me in celebration,
And God began to pull, from where He sat.
You pulled me too. The not-seen was now seen:

The end-result a case of God-confusion.
Because who else could do a thing like that?
Because you found me somewhere in-between,

God stepped aside, for you, and it was done.
And so the grave-clothes, and your welcome mat.
Pull me up. The not-seen was now seen.

Who would have thought? The son in imitation:
And I come stumbling out into the sunlight.
Because you found me somewhere in-between,
You pulled me up, like roots, as was foreseen.

Samson and Delilah

1.

Once the scratch is scratched, the eyes have turned;
Once the memory wants to be returned;

Once the ritual's made, the clearing cleared;
Once the secret's located and bared;

Once it was difficult to tell which one was who,
Once we were all we ever thought to do.

Once I was young, and love was not diminished;
Once, I turned; I saw her, and I was astonished.

Once eyes were gouged, I had a different strength,
One based on introspection, not on length.

Belief is a shining thing, or a lock of hair,
A change in the psyche cutting off forever.

You like to think you can go back. You can't.
She taught me both to want, and not to want.

2.

He taught me both to want, and not to want.
You like to think you can go back. You can't:

A change in the psyche cutting off forever.
Belief is a shining thing, or a lock of hair,

One based on introspection, not on length.
Once eyes were gouged, I had a different strength.

Once, I turned; I saw him, and I was astonished.
Once, I was young, and love was not diminished.

Once we were all we ever thought to do,
Once it was difficult to tell which one was who.

Once the secret's located and bare,
Once the ritual's made, the clearing cleared,

Once the memory wants to be returned,
Once the scratch is scratched, the eyes have turned.

Brides of Christ

My first urge was to laugh, there at the door.
A Bride of Christ received me looking for my group.
It was the surprise, and the halo that she wore:
She pointed me to a house just down the Cape.

But, when the Brides of Christ arrived at dinner,
All wearing haloes like a children's party,
I wanted to be one. They laughed, got a tray,
And focused on their main dish, sides, their silver

Headwear bedraggled like a Christmas tree.
But it was spring. The best time to be a bride.

We were at a camp, so all of us were trying
To be remade. Plain, middle-aged, I wouldn't be lying
If I said we were jealous of each sparkling braid
Fashioned out of wonder and of pity.

Peter

You were that kind of guy. The kind to think
That you were better than the others. That's
The curse, you see. I knew that you would blame
Circumstances and the atmosphere.
That's how it is: You are what you most fear.
You think you know your shining, private name:
You don't. It is the language of your secrets.
You couldn't believe that you'd deny. To think

That this was you! Inside your robes, the feeling
Of guilt that shamed; your goodness was inferred.
You have many ways to shape how you are weak.
For example, you must bear the blame, the word
You know you didn't say. This is your failing.
Yet God gives you a do-over, once you speak.

Karma

By the end, you will have suffered from it all:
At first you didn't understand why people
That you worked with would think about you, quibble
With how you lived your life. Now you know fall
And rise, how a life has more to do with lies.
How jealousy is understandable,
Revenge the toothpick in the gums, to trouble
Even you. There is a bitterness in ways
Of seeing: those heavy, layered wines; the bread
Poisoned. *Come, sit down. My favorite is the crust.*
It's not that the last supper was the last;
It was the day that it revealed that even
The good guys were impure. How they were lost
And resisted giving up what they were given.

Judas

How many times does the lamb die? How many
Times do you dismiss that your calculation
Will make a change? Perhaps you don't think any.
It may be that you risk humiliation
Because you think a shekel more or less
Is like the rough, lost greeting of a kiss:
So what. You never thought it would be terror.
You never thought his goodness was in error.
So why? You can't explain it to yourself.
In the end, the heaviness of your betrayal
Is all you think about; hangs on the wall.
You move from non-belief to your belief
The way that others pin their character
On ruin, then look up. The tears are pure.

What Fresh Hell Is This?

As if it's not enough for hell to be
Outdated, eternal, and reminiscent.
Even so, you recognize its current.
The *fresh* is just surprise. The vicious bully;
Lead in the water. Someone's bureaucratic
Way of punishing a subordinate.
Hell can figure a coordinate
On a graph that seems both fair and democratic.
Explosive like a migraine, sunburst-static.

You have free choice, but always the choice is wrong:
A game show with a trick. Sick about everything—
Your life, your lot—you refuse the kind of awe
That hell requires. Worm-thing stuck in its craw:
The minute you are kind, it eats you raw.

VI.

Over the Hill

Over the Hill

"I never knew where the hill *was*,"
a remark made in passing.

Because there never was a hill,
You never knew just where it was.
It could have been that stone, that pebble.

But first you had to make life level:
To go to school, get work, not pause.
Because you thought there *was* a hill,

You had your child, sent *him* to school.
You followed all the cold, gray laws.
It could have been that stone, that pebble,

That made you fall. An obscure rule.
This setback made you realize—
Don't worry so about the hill!—

That sometimes it's inconsequential
What you prize and do not prize.
It could have been that stone, that pebble,

Or maybe it was monumental.
You couldn't tell with clouded eyes.
What was that thing? Was it a hill?
From here, it looked more like a pebble.

What Will Happen Next

When John F. Kennedy died, my mother dropped a dish,
And the news was in black and white. I know
It's always dropping one thing and picking up
Another. Then, I thought there was a tiger
Living in my toy box, at night. One day, it was gone,
Ghostly, outgrown, like footie pajamas. When the mall
Near my house opened, I dressed up to go
With my friend, and we walked up and down, looking.
Now, the last stores are coughing their last breath.
In the '80s people wondered if computers would last,
And now it doesn't take much to make people
Hold hands with a predator. I always thought
I knew what was coming, like the time I got in the car
With someone who turned out to be a stranger.
Sometimes it can turn out all right,
But some people are not so lucky
Like the family at Walmart delivering themselves,
With joy about their boon of new outfits,
To a kidnapper. The Homecoming king of my class
Died shortly after graduation, and a friend
With Cleopatra hair as perfect as a wig
Died on a motorcycle: no helmet. Why them?
Each time is just another choice.
When my fourth grade teacher's husband died,
We lived in her grief, like a cloud, picking glue-patches
Off our hands. We could not have known why.
We just knew we were sad, all of us, together.
I was always afraid of change: junior high school,
Having a locker, thinking I would be crushed
As shyness often is, by the powerful.
The first day I brought a lunch box, but no one else did,
And I had to put my pretty lunch box away.
It was a sack lunch now. When teachers noticed me,
Told me I would be someone, I was surprised.

I am still surprised by what other people think.
I might win a national award
But fall down the stairs and skin my knees,
Because I was not paying attention.
Years later, students were talking on the phone
On the way to class: and I knew the world had changed.
How do you tell the difference between sorrow, and rage,
And hope? What makes some contented
To do the same as everyone else? For me,
The gangplank and the diving board can look the same.
That's been the trouble all my life.
I'm aghast when people accuse me
Of things I did not do, but I'll make a new empire,
Happily, absorbed, by the sand.
Some days, I try to find the girl
Who heard her mother drop a dish,
The plate breaking on the floor,
And she's there, I almost see her,
The moment before the shot.

Not Giving Baklava

To my friend, Agha Shahid Ali,
after reading my manuscript
"Why I'm Giving You Baklava"

My friend Shahid told me *not* giving baklava would make people wonder.
I laughed out loud. I didn't believe him, wanted the sample of wonder.

We watched Katharine Hepburn and Bollywood. He said we were a couple
Because we looked good together; doubting, people looked with ample wonder.

He always made me feel—in the faculty dining room—that he was a party.
I looked like Dido Merwin, and Shahid shook his head, *The simple wonder.*

He died only a few years later, from his mother's brain disease.
Those days, he read my manuscript, eliminated dappled wonder.

He said that no adult should be so pure, so free of heartache, loss.
It was better to have been hurt, to have tasted the apple of wonder.

Come back changed, he said. Now, when I look at the manuscript,
Each edit seems miraculous, absence praying to the steeple of wonder.

And I think of his voice on the phone, even though he lived close by,
Reading new poems, finding something to grapple in wonder.

He told me we liked the same type, when he met my husband.
He explained, "Kim, this is the difference between *wander* and *wonder*."

Why People in Their Fifties Read Mystery Books

Because the world is solvable; because
Human complications have a glow
When they are not your own; because what *is*
Finds all its shameful roots in what you know,
But you don't want to know. Spite, envy, and greed:
They run the plots the way they do in life.
(You trick yourself into thinking that to read
Is to escape; here you just see the knife.)
Because the habits in a character—
Like drink, or infidelity—enliven,
Don't bring the horror that they should. Ah, layman,
Because of sex, cash, settling an old score.
Because true evil is a predator.
In middle age, these reasons all mean more.

Campfire

They died together, working on the truck.
They didn't realize the closed-in space.
They didn't realize, in oil and grease,
How tired they were. They curled into physique.

When I heard of a family, dead, in Mexico,
I thought of you. How you went on,
Having lost your husband and your son.
Your house was weekly clean. You made it so.

I entered in, at a different part of time.
You blended into church, and special days,
With your sister. Both you and she reorganized.
The young don't understand the earlier gleam

Of sorrow, but accept the "who will be there,
Who will not." It was over in their sleep.
You, awake: the company you keep
Will be those on this side of poison air,

Not ones who holding wrenches and despair,
And words, and good-night everyone,
Are wandering the invisible horizon.
They want a place to stop, and build a campfire.

Being 86

As time goes on, you get more distance: true.
As things reorganize, you understand.
Of course, you realize it is not you,

Even when it is. Even something borrowed, blue,
Is just your take within the marriage legend.
As time goes on, you get more distance. True,

You get things started. True, they go on now,
And you are somewhere else. You are at an end.
Of course, you realize it is not you.

Just a few bars of music, or a hello.
People always said that you were kind.
As time goes on, you get more distance: true.

Your devotion to ideals is all you knew.
(Perhaps, in time, anonymous is signed.)
Of course, you realize it is not you.

Now, that you're here, it's clear what will ensue:
In falling to the future, you will find
As time goes on, you get more distance: true.
Of course, you realize it is not you.

Spoils

Some really sad things happened. We went on.
We always like to think we were our best.
Sometimes we only see things later on:

The vicious bullying we didn't comment on
(We were sidetracked with the personal, we confessed).
Some really sad things happened. We went on.

On a certain level, when we peeked to watch it happen,
It was satisfying. Good, like being kissed.
Sometimes we only see things later on,

The way she was always kind to us. When she was broken,
We didn't realize we had regressed.
Some really sad things happened. We went on.

It was best she went away—a myth, unspoken.
Her husband's heart attack made us feel lost.
Sometimes we only see things later on,

But prefer these thoughts remain in contemplation.
We want the spoils, but do not want the cost.
Some really sad things happened. We went on.
Sometimes we only see things later on.

The Artist

Born to find his metaphor,
He used to play out in the woods.
He doesn't do that anymore.

He went to school, found more and more
The *can't*s, and *don't*s, and *must*s, and *should*s.
Born to find his metaphor,

And live outside the either/or
(A way to tear the rules to shreds),
He doesn't do that anymore.

On the Enneagram a 4,
He was a captive to his moods.
Born to find his metaphor,

An ice cream cup with flimsy oar
(Quixote-ed verisimilitudes!),
He doesn't do that anymore;

He doesn't know what it was for.
Merlot relieves the platitudes.
Born to find his metaphor,
He doesn't do that anymore.

Why Sisyphus Isn't a Woman

Because it wouldn't be mythological,
Just life. What woman hasn't pushed a rock,
Or two or ten? It's not an obstacle,
But a way of navigating. No shock.
Instead, it's the efficient way to push
While also writing a book or raising a child.

Because no one would be interested in it.

Because if it weren't a boulder, but a system
Rigged to keep her back, and she weren't a lamb,
We would see the wrongness festered in it.

Because this Sisyphus complained too much,
And drove the other heroes almost wild.

Because when you change what's most obvious—
The central figure—it is away from us.

You Can't Go Back

"You can't go back," my mother always said.
But human nature does the opposite.
(Of course, this happens, but inside your head.)

Unspill your coffee? Leave your words unsaid?
The jeans from years ago will suddenly fit!
"You can't go back," my mother always said,

And she was right. The dead are not undead,
And traumas still will need a tourniquet.
(Of course, this happens, but inside your head.)

You want your moments cut and edited.
You want the bliss, and not the deep regret.
"You can't go back," my mother always said.

The trick is to remember what you had
And simultaneously forgive, forget.
(Of course, this happens, but inside your head.)

It is never quite in balance, this method
Of loving who you were, and you aren't yet.
"You can't go back," my mother always said.
(Of course, this happens, but inside your head.)

.

www.ingramcontent.com/pod-product-compliance
Lightning Source LLC
LaVergne TN
LVHW021618080426
835510LV00019B/2635